SLAY THE SYNOPSIS

CLARISSA **KAE**
KAYLEE **BALDWIN**
ADAM **BERG**

SLAY THE SYNOPSIS

Writing a Synopsis Like a Pro

CLARISSA KAE   KAYLEE BALDWIN   ADAM BERG

CARPE VITAM
PRESS LLC

CONTENTS

INTRODUCTION

You poured your soul into writing an amazing, unputdownable story that you can't wait to see in bookstores and in readers' hands. Every word matters. Every character motivation is honed to a perfect degree. The kisses are scorching. And that twist? It's delicious enough to make people flip back to the beginning to see where they missed the clues.

But there's just one eensy-weensy little problem ...

The agents or editors you're querying are asking for a synopsis.

They want you to take your 100,000-word masterpiece and summarize it in about 500 words. It's a harder task than writing the entire book in the first place.

What storylines do you include? How do you prove you can tell a satisfying story with such a small amount of page real estate? How will agents/editors understand the full emotional impact of the twist ending if they read a spoiler of it before diving into the book?

It feels like taking a lush, dimensional painting down to the barest, faintest sketch lines and expecting viewers to see your vision.

How in the world would that help an agent or editor decide to read more of your book?

We understand that this isn't an easy ask, while also seeing the importance of it. We want you to succeed and learn how to handle writing synopses like a pro.

Additionally, it's important for writers who plan to self-publish to learn how to write a synopsis. This skill can become an invaluable tool in your writing toolbox to improve your storytelling and maybe even help you write faster.

In this book, we're going to break down:

- Why a synopsis is important.
- How synopsis writing can improve your story.
- Synopsis writing methods.
- Tips for success.

1

WHY DO SYNOPSES MATTER?

IF WE DON'T UNDERSTAND what value they have in the first place, it's hard to get motivated to learn how to write one. First, though, let's dive into the stripped-down, nuts-and-bolts of what a synopsis is.

WHAT IS A SYNOPSIS?

A synopsis is a one-page, single-spaced summary (or approximately 500 words) of your entire book.

How is this different from a query?

A query is designed to whet the reader's appetite, leave them hanging, and entice them to read more. You give just enough information to lure them in.

A synopsis, on the other hand, is to show that you have a solid and cohesive story, including an ending that makes sense. You don't leave the reader hanging. You spoil all the good and juicy bits. If you leave it unresolved, the synopsis will only irritate the agent or editor reading it.

. . .

I have to spoil my own book?

Yes. The entire point of a synopsis is to demonstrate that your book has a satisfying narrative arc from beginning to end. I can't tell you how often a book with fabulous writing and a killer premise starts to fall apart halfway through. The overarching question of the synopsis is: Can you tell a good story?

If it makes you feel any better about spoiling your story, though, think about how much time it takes from query, to requested pages and synopsis, to full-request by an agent or editor. Months may pass in this process, and agents and editors will read a lot of other manuscripts in the meantime. By the time they get to reading your requested manuscript, it's likely they'll have completely forgotten the twist or unique plot element you revealed in your synopsis, and get to experience it as a fresh reader.

What if I plan on self-publishing? Is this relevant to me?

Absolutely. One of the most important pieces of advice I give writers—even seasoned ones—is this: Write your synopsis before you write your book.

> PRO-TIP: Write your synopsis before you write your book.

This will ensure you have a satisfying narrative arc. You'll know where your story is going and what you're trying to say. Writing it before drafting your book doesn't mean that it's set in stone, but it will give you a road map to follow as you start your story.

This can help stave off writer's block or a general uncertainty with your story, as you'll already know in which general direction you're heading. Though I can't promise this, of course, many writers I know who use this method are able to write their first drafts faster because they spend less time trying to figure out where the story is going (or rewriting when they realize they've taken a tangent or written themselves into a corner) and more time drafting.

I would suggest this for *all* writers opening up a blank document to start a new story.

I would also encourage *all* writers to write a synopsis (or refine their prewritten one) once they've finished drafting their books. There's nothing like writing a concise summary of your book to realize that your hook isn't strong enough, your characters lack motivation, or your story has veered way off course and you never brought it back on track.

In the end, our readers want a good story. And writing a synopsis for your book will make it a stronger story, whether you do it before or after drafting.

IN SUMMARY

SYNOPSES ARE IMPORTANT TO AGENTS/EDITORS BECAUSE:

- They reveal the entire narrative arc of the story.
- They ensure realistic character arcs and motivations.
- They make sure it's not the same, retold story they've seen hundreds of times.

SYNOPSES ARE IMPORTANT TO AUTHORS BECAUSE:

- They reveal plot holes.
- They show gaps in character motivation.
- A lack of narrative structure becomes apparent.
- They make sure your story is unique enough.

2

WRITING A SYNOPSIS: THE 5-STEP METHOD

We're going to break down two different methods for writing a synopsis: The five-step method and the word vomit (aka stream of consciousness) method.

With the five-step method, we are going to begin with our scaffolding by isolating the most important aspects of our story:

- The status quo
- The inciting incident
- Rising action/developments
- The crisis
- The resolution

These five points will drive the arc of our synopsis, proving that you've written a cohesive and compelling story. Let's break them down a little further.

1. STATUS QUO

This is where your main character is at when the book starts, before their world changes. What does "normal" life look like for your protagonist?

- Questions to answer: Who is my main character? What do they want? What is their goal?

These are the elements that will drive character motivation and spring them into the plot of the novel. It can be tempting, especially in a full-cast novel, to include every character. But there's not enough space for that in a synopsis. Your novel may have a lot of really important characters or multiple point-of-view characters, but it should still have a protagonist, or the person who is the main driver of the plot and will undergo the most change.

> PRO-TIP: Capitalize a character's entire name the first time they are mentioned in the synopsis.

A synopsis will be concise. Ignore the side storylines. If a detail isn't showing the main, overarching conflict, then it's unnecessary for the synopsis.

Let's go back to the scaffolding analogy. When builders are creating the framework for your house, they are not worried about drywall and carpet yet. Those things will come. But if the overall structure isn't correct, then the entire house falls apart.

If your story starts in medias res (or right in the middle of the story/action), you can still include the relevant details of their life. For all intents and purposes of the synopsis, their current state is the status quo.

WRITING EXERCISE: STATUS QUO

1. Pick a favorite book or movie. Answer these questions about it:
    a. Who is the main character?
    b. What do they want?
    c. What does "status quo" look like in their world?

2. Answer these same questions for your WIP or an idea you're brainstorming for a future WIP.
    a. Who is my main character?
    b. What do they want?
    c. What does "status quo" look like in their world?

2. INCITING INCIDENT

The inciting incident is what happens in your story that changes the trajectory of your protagonist's path.

In *Pride and Prejudice*, the inciting incident is when Mr. Bingley and Mr. Darcy move to Netherfield Park. It is the event that disrupts the normal state of events.

When you think of your story, you can imagine your character chugging along on train-track A. Maybe they're unhappily stuck in a rut. Or maybe they are living their best life. Either way, they have very little indication that they won't always be on Track A.

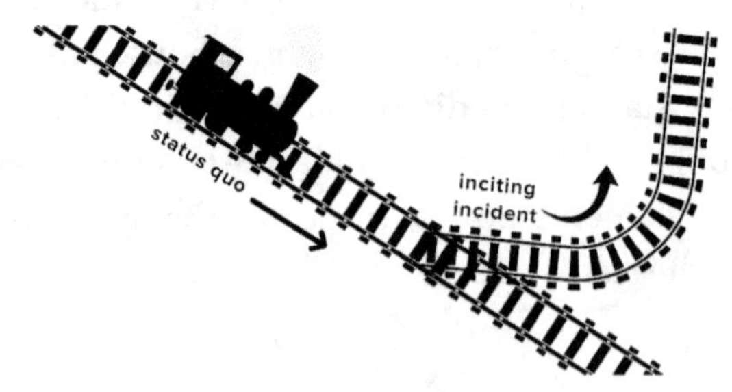

. . .

But then with a crank of a lever, their train is flipped to Track B, and the entire direction of their life, and what they expected, is different. Remaining on track A isn't as compelling a story as seeing what's in store down Track B.

What is Harry Potter without the letter inviting him to Hogwarts? Or *The Hunger Games* without Katniss volunteering to take her sister's place in the games?

That crank of the lever is the inciting incident. It needs to be strong enough to cause disruption, and compelling enough to keep your reader engaged.

If you are writing your synopsis and realize you don't have a clear inciting incident, you may need to reevaluate how your story starts.

WRITING EXERCISE: INCITING INCIDENT

1. List 10 inciting incidents from books and movies. In what ways do these moments change the trajectory of the story?

2. What is the inciting incident in your WIP? How does this incident change things for your main character? Is it compelling and interesting?

3. RISING ACTION AND DEVELOPMENTS

Here is where our plot steps in and gets to shine. We've established character, their normal world, and how their normal world is being disrupted.

Now we get to dive into the fun (and most difficult) part: What is actually happening in this story?

When you think of rising action, picture a graph that looks a bit like a hill. We are going to focus on the circled part on the image below.

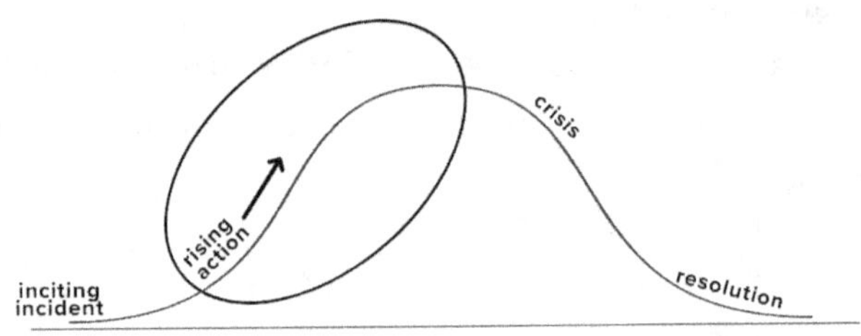

Your character is being thrust into new, unfamiliar circumstances. They have their goal in hand and we give a sense of what might happen if they don't achieve that goal.

From there, tell us about the obstacles keeping them from their goal and what is keeping them from going back to the status quo. This portion of your synopsis will make up the bulk of it. As a reminder, you are focusing on the main conflict and main character(s), leaving out any side storylines.

Additionally, you want to make sure you are ramping up the tension. Think of that arc above and picture your reader sitting on a rollercoaster. There's that anticipatory feeling at the beginning, when the rollercoaster is clicking up, up, up on the tracks. It's setting up the wild ride you're about to go on.

Do the same with your story. Make sure you're building toward something that your reader can't wait to get to.

There's a reason this is the tricky part, though. First you have to parse out what the most compelling plot points are. Second, you have to make sure it creates a cohesive representation of your story arc. Third, it has to demonstrate directional confidence—meaning, you know where this story is going and how you are going to take us there.

WRITING EXERCISE: RISING ACTION 1

1. If your WIP is already written, do a bullet point for every chapter and answer these questions:
   - What happens in this scene?
   - What is the conflict?
   - How does this scene relate to the overarching story conflict?
   - What new thing did we learn from this scene?
   - Is it imperative I include it in my synopsis? Why?
   - Put an asterisk beside those necessary plot points.

WRITING EXERCISE: RISING ACTION 2

Draw an arc as pictured below. Plot the points on your arc that lead to the crisis moment.

This will help you to visualize your story in a way that will show you if your tension is ramping up or not.

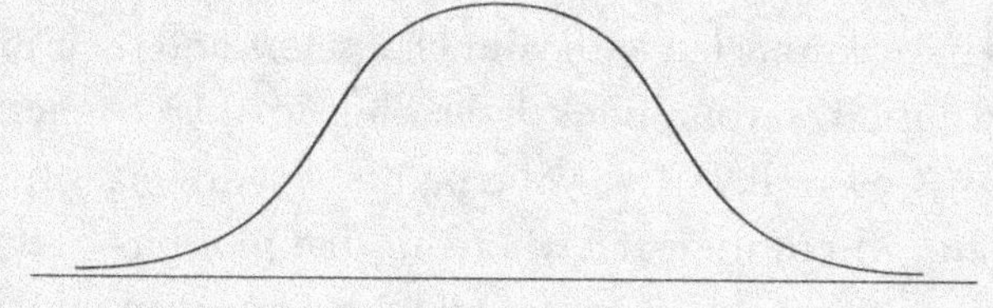

WRITING EXERCISE: RISING ACTION 3

Think of your book as a three-act play. At the end of each act, your character should go through a door of no return. Act II will show the consequences of going through the door of Act I, as well as actions taken to meet the protagonist's goal.

Act I	Act II	Act III

4. CRISIS

You may have heard the crisis point of the story called other things—the all-is-lost moment, the dark night of the soul, the climax—but it all comes down to this: The moment your character has failed to achieve their goal. Or they achieved their goal and it has the opposite effect than what they expected.

This is the moment most of the story is leading toward.

Facing the bad guy and realizing, as he has you at the brink of death, that you're just not strong enough after all.

Getting the job you always wanted but realizing it means you'll have to move away from the new love of your life.

Learning that despite Headquarters' best efforts to bring you home, you will be lost in space forever.

Your story's crisis will be emotionally resonant when your readers have connected with your characters and their journey.

And just like your book is leading to this moment, your synopsis is as well. All of your points are driving you to this very point, where we learn where all that plot has been taking us. Readers crave the unexpected, with one essential caveat. It all has to make sense within the context of the story we've already been told.

If your crisis comes out of nowhere in your synopsis, it will be easy to assume the story is this way as well. We are taking someone on a guided path through a windy, intricate garden maze with only a few markers to show the way. Too many markers will distract from the overall aesthetic; too few and we'll get lost.

WRITING EXERCISE: CRISIS

1. Go back to your favorite movie or book. What is the crisis point in that story? If you rewatch or reread it, were there any clues leading to this point? What were they?

2. Write down the crisis moment in your WIP. Go back to your bullet-point scene list from the "Writing Exercise: Rising Action" section and highlight the scenes that point to this moment.

5. RESOLUTION

This is the final stretch of both our synopsis and our story. This is Mr. Darcy coming to Longbourn for one final chance at winning Elizabeth's hand. It's the final, last-ditch effort to save humanity. It's the successful capture of the real murderer.

Your characters have hit rock bottom and there is no place to go but up, whether that's practically or emotionally.

In the synopsis, this is where you will give the final, satisfying details of your story. Including twists or unexpected revelations and the book's very last plot point. If writing this synopsis is like eating a cake, then you are licking your plate clean, leaving no crumbs behind.

Lay it all on the page.

WRITING EXERCISE: RESOLUTION

1. How does your favorite movie/book end? What about that ending makes this book or movie stand out to you? Is it unique to other movies/books? If not, what then makes it so compelling that it's your favorite? What details and emotions does it stir in you?

2. How does your WIP end? What emotion do you want the reader to feel when they close your book? Play with word choices to see if you can convey that emotion in your synopsis.

PULL IT ALL TOGETHER

You've answered all the questions for your book, now it's time to pull it all together and pare it down to the most essential points, while still retaining your good storytelling ability. A bullet-pointed list of the plot isn't enough to entice someone to read the book. What this does, instead, is give you a framework to then fill in with more details, good writing, transitions, flow, and a sense of tone, mood, and writing style.

Once it is polished, it is ready to go.

3

WRITING A SYNOPSIS: WORD VOMIT METHOD

MAYBE YOU READ the last chapter, and you thought: No, nopity, nope. That method is not for me. And that is totally valid. Our brains all work so differently, and while a structured, outline format might work for one type of writer, it will feel like torture to another.

And so we present to you: word vomit.

Another way to word it that is maybe a little more pleasant is "stream-of-consciousness writing" or "unfiltered drafting." This method may appeal to pantsers, who thrive on writing stories by the seat of their pants.

It may also work effectively for authors who want to write a synopsis *before* they begin drafting their manuscript.

THE BLANK SHEET

For this method, you'll start with a blank sheet of paper.

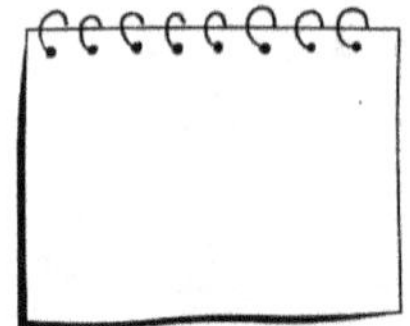

Some people prefer to put pen to paper for this, to have that additional connectivity with their story. Other people type so much faster than they can handwrite, and they need to let their fingers fly over the keys.

And then you answer this core question:

What is my story about?

Don't think about length or structure. Instead, every thought that comes into your mind will go on the paper. Don't filter yourself, but instead let those creative juices run free.

When you get done, you may have ten pages describing what your story is about. Maybe it reads like a dry, laundry list of events. That's okay. Because ten pages is a lot more manageable to summarize than an entire novel.

And from here, we're going to make it shine.

WRITING EXERCISE

What is your book about? Write the entire plot from beginning to end.

FILTERING THE UNFILTERED

Okay, this might hurt a little. But we've got to take the solid block of stream-of-consciousness writing and chisel it down into something with shape (and a whole lot of white space).

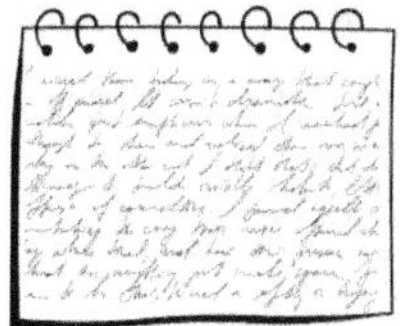

It may help here to refer to the 5-step guide for synopsis writing in the last chapter to make sure you include the necessary elements of a synopsis: the status quo, the inciting incident, rising action and developments, the crisis, and the resolution. If you go in this direction, have fun with it! Maybe get five different-colored highlighters out and color in each portion. Or cut it up and lay the pieces out to see which ones can be removed and which ones stay.

If the thought of that 5-step guide makes you want to crawl into a hole where synopses don't exist, then you're going to have to operate off of instinct and your knowledge of good storytelling.

If you have those highlighters, go through and mark the parts of your story that are the most important for capturing character and narrative arc. Make sure there is a recognizable beginning, middle, and end. Then ruthlessly cut any other details that aren't absolutely necessary. You are going to pare this thing down to one page, which means only the most essential details can stay.

But always keep this in mind as you cut: beginning, middle, and end. You need to showcase these three portions of your story in a way that is compelling, taut, and engaging. Above all, your synopsis is showing that you can tell a really good story.

WRITING EXERCISE

1. Get 5 highlighters and assign a color to each of these elements: status quo, inciting incident, rising action/developments, crisis, and resolution. Go through your pages and mark it up.

2. Or read through each page and start deleting or crossing out plot points that aren't necessary to the synopsis. Remember, we're only following the protagonist and their journey. If you've included information about side characters or side plots, those aren't needed for a synopsis.

TAKING IT TO THE SENTENCE LEVEL

Once you have your synopsis mostly streamlined and set, then you can pay attention to the micro-level details at a sentence-level. Polish that stream of consciousness so it sounds as good as the writing in your book sounds. Every word needs to carry its weight, since you can only have so few.

WRITING EXERCISE

Go through each individual sentence of your pared-down synopsis. Are you using powerful verbs? Is your word choice conveying tone and emotion? Does one sentence flow seamlessly into the next?

✓ MY SYNOPSIS CHECKLIST

- ☐ I reveal the beginning, middle, and end of my story.
- ☐ I have focused on my protagonist.
- ☐ I have included the status quo, the inciting incident, rising action and developments, the crisis, and the resolution.
- ☐ It is one page, or no more than 500-600 words.
- ☐ The characters' entire names are capitalized when first mentioned.
- ☐ The synopsis is written in 3rd-person, present tense.

4

TIPS FOR SUCCESS

There are a few things you can do to make your synopsis a step above the rest.

1. Have someone who hasn't read your book read the synopsis and give you feedback on it. Since we know our entire story, front to back, it is easy to fill in any blanks. Same for our critique partners who have read our books. Someone who has no familiarity with the story, though, can tell you which parts were confusing to them. This will be invaluable feedback for you to consider in your final edits.

2. Look at the publisher or agent's website for their formatting instructions. Some will prefer one page, single spaced. Others will want double-spaced pages. It's easy enough to change formatting, and it goes a long way in submissions to show that you can follow directions.

. . .

3. Try to only mention two characters by name (three max) or else it can get too confusing. Only discuss characters *essential* to the main conflict.

4. Leave out backstory and dialogue. Save those for your manuscript.

5. Capitalize characters' names the first time they are mentioned. Include age if relevant.

6. Use tight and stripped-down language. This is not the place for purple prose or wordiness. You can convey tone via succinct and specific word choice.

7. Make sure you're *telling* the story, not *selling* the story. This isn't a query where you leave them hanging and hungry for more. The hunger for more will come from realizing that you are a phenomenal storyteller.

8. Give your synopsis a rest and come back to it after a few days. You will have a clear mind to read your synopsis with and will see more mistakes that way.

9. Don't give up! Take as many breaks as you need. Get all the feedback you require. It will come together.

CONCLUSION

Writing a synopsis will require a lot of effort, but the results are worth it in the end. The process of writing a synopsis will not only get your book submission-ready, it will help develop your storytelling skills. Once you start to see the structure of a story, you can't go back. You'll notice it in the movies you're watching, the books you're reading, and it'll be there when you sit down to write your next manuscript.

In the end, it doesn't matter what method you use or when you write it. Perhaps you want to write your synopsis as you go. Or you think having it written before you even start your book will give you a lot of direction. Maybe you don't want to be tied into anything that even remotely resembles an outline, and you know that waiting until the story is done is the best time for you to write it.

There is no right or wrong timing for writing your synopsis.

Additionally, you should experiment with different methods and figure out what works for you. You may be all-in on a five-step guide or 100% a word-vomit writer. Many of us will create a hybrid method that involves portions of both. If one way isn't working for you, try another. Don't give up, though. Take a break, then come back to it again.

What we've given you here are tools to help you tackle something that can feel overwhelming or unmanageable. Taken in smaller chunks, a synopsis isn't quite as bad as it seems at the outset. Don't let your concern or dread over synopsis writing limit your opportunities.

And maybe the best part of having a written synopsis? When someone asks you what your story is about, you won't freeze and forget what words even are. You'll have a streamlined and concise summary of your story right there in your head, and that'll give you all the confidence you need to answer that question.

Take control of your publishing journey with this focused self-publishing workbook. Learn how to move from finished manuscript to a polished, market-ready book with clarity and confidence. We'll cover positioning, blurbs, cover decisions, formatting, and distribution, along with practical strategies for building your author brand and reaching readers through platforms like Amazon.

Whether you're launching your first book or leveling up your next release, you'll gain actionable steps, avoid common pitfalls, and end up with a clear roadmap. Perfect for fiction and nonfiction authors ready to publish professionally—on your timeline, your terms.

Available on Amazon

ABOUT THE AUTHORS

Kaylee Baldwin's love of all things books and reading led her to graduate from Arizona State University with a degree in English. She writes romantic comedies with a side of angst (and literary references, because she's a book nerd at heart.) She has worked as an editor for over six years, helping authors bring hundreds of manuscripts to publication, and spent over ten years helping run the Storymakers Writers Conference.

She lives in Arizona with her family, and adores traveling, finding gluten-free recipes that are actually delicious, and pretending she's going to read all the books she buys.

You can find her online on Instagram @kayleebaldwinbooks or www.kayleebaldwin.com.

Clarissa Kae draws from her Spanish and Mexican heritage as a fresh voice in historical and women's fiction. Former president of her local California Writers Club, Clarissa has spent her early career with Pitch Perfect Conference, Writer's Digest and

Equus. She's dedicated countless hours to mentoring fellow authors before founding Carpe Vitam Press.

With numerous awards to her name, she continues to honor the timeless role of storyteller, weaving myth and history into evocative, emotionally rich narratives.

She holds a degree in animal and veterinary genetics and carries a lifelong devotion to animals and their welfare—but nothing gives her more joy than her family and beloved Friesians.

You can find Clarissa on Instagram @clarissa_kae or at www.clarissakae.com.

Adam Berg is a real human boy and not a figment of his dog's imagination. He started his career in sketch comedy, spending seven years writing and acting for Studio C. Now he works for JK Studios. His love of writing has pushed him to explore TV, film, gaming articles, and YA fantasy novels.

Born and raised in Utah, he spends his days jotting down dumb jokes and annoying his maltipoo with relentless kisses. If you Google him, just know he's not actually worth 10 million dollars (yet?) or is a 50-year-old Swedish film director (yet).

Find him online at:

Instagram: @heyadamberg

Threads: @heyadamberg

Twitter: @theadamberg

Learn more about Carpe Vitam Press at www.carpevitampress.com or @carpevitampress on Instagram.

ALSO BY KAYLEE BALDWIN

Enchanted Forresters

Me and Mr. Just Right

Rosie and the Beast Next Door

Amelia and Her Prince Charming

Evie and The Big Bad Bodyguard

Christmas

Snowed In at Jingle Falls

Take My Heart

Diamond Cove

A Summer Mismatch

A Wedding Mismatch

Billionaire Cove

Her Billionaire Rival

Her Billionaire Heartthrob

ALSO BY CLARISSA KAE

Prince of Death

Reign of Mercy

Reign of Chaos (Winter 2026)

Time Slip Novels

Of Ink And Sea

Women's Fiction

Pieces To Mend

Once And Future Wife Series

Once And Future Wife

Victorian Retellings

A Dark Beauty, Beauty & the Beast

Cinders Like Glass, Cinderella

A Stolen Heart, Robin Hood

Taming Christmas, Taming of the Shrew (standalone)

A Light So Fleeting, Rapunzel (novella)

The Wolf of Heathclove Manor (novella)

ALSO BY ADAM BERG

Rainbringer

The Broken Pantheon

Straight on till Dusk (novella)

The Emperor's New Armor (novella)

www.ingramcontent.com/pod-product-compliance
Lightning Source LLC
LaVergne TN
LVHW020050110826
845155LV00029B/710

* 9 7 8 1 9 5 4 6 1 5 9 6 0 *